Super Science Projects About

Light and Optics

Allan B. Cobb

the rosen publishing group's
rosen central
new york

To my mom and dad for always encouraging my love of science and nature.

Published in 2000 by The Rosen Publishing Group, Inc.
29 East 21st Street, New York, NY 10010

First Edition

Library of Congress Cataloging-in-Publication Data

Cobb, Allan B.
    Super science projects about light and optics / Allan B. Cobb.
        p. cm. — (Psyched for science)
    Includes bibliographical references and index.
    Summary: Introduces basic principles of light and optics through hands-on activities and experiments.
    ISBN 0-8239-3177-3
    1. Optics—Experiments—Juvenile literature. 2. Light—Experiments—Juvenile literature. 3. Science projects—Juvenile literature. [1. Optics—Experiments. 2. Light—Experiments. 3. Experiments. 4. Science projects.] I. Title. II. Series.

RC365.C63 1999
535'.078—dc21

                                                                        99-051305

Manufactured in the United States of America

contents

Light and Optics

Light is everywhere. You turn on lights in your home, there are lights at stores and at school, and at night cars turn their lights on. The sun is also a source of light. Even though it is 93 million miles away (150 million km), we see its light and feel the energy from its rays. The stars that we see at night emit light also. Their light has been traveling for hundreds, thousands, or even more years to reach Earth. Light travels through the vacuum of space at 186,282 miles per second (299,792 km/sec).

What we see as light is only a small part of what's called the electromagnetic spectrum. The electromagnetic spectrum is made up of gamma rays, X rays, radio waves, infrared waves, visible light, ultraviolet rays, and microwaves, which are short electromagnetic waves. What we see as light is actually made up of different colors—the colors of the rainbow.

Because light travels in waves, it has certain properties. A beam of light travels in a straight line unless something affects its path. These properties of light make it possible to see our reflection in a mirror and to make telescopes that magnify distant objects.

In this book you will explore some of the properties of light. You will have an opportunity to investigate how light travels in a straight line, how it bounces off surfaces, how light bends and slows down as it passes through materials, how it can be separated into different colors, and how the intensity of light changes with distance. After exploring the properties of light, you will apply some of the concepts that you have learned. You will also study lenses: how they form an image of an object at some distance and how it changes with image distance. Then you will explore how a series of two lenses are combined to form a telescope that magnifies distant objects.

The experiments in this book provide detailed instructions for getting started. Beyond that, they depend on your observations. Each activity has its own instructions and safety warnings. After completing these activities, you will have a better idea of what light is and how light waves travel through different materials.

1 How Light Travels

Light comes from many different sources—the sun, stars, lightbulbs, and flames. Light is a form of electromagnetic radiation (energy that is transmitted through free space or through a material). Light and other electromagnetic radiation travel in waves. These waves are much like waves in the ocean.

Electromagnetic waves can be measured by their wavelength. Wavelength is the distance between identical points in two waves that come one after the other. The light we see is actually only a narrow range of wavelengths within the entire electromagnetic spectrum.

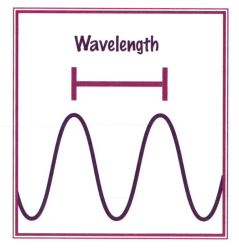
Wavelength

As light travels in waves, the light waves move in a particular direction. This direction can change as the light waves come into contact with objects. For example, when light strikes a shiny surface, it is reflected. When light strikes a mirror at an angle, it is reflected off the surface at an angle. This is called the angle of reflection.

In this activity, you will explore how light travels in straight lines and how its direction changes by reflection.

Experiment #1

What You Need

- 3 index cards
- Modeling clay
- Scissors
- A flashlight
- A shoe box
- 2 small mirrors
- Tape

What You'll Do

#1   In each index card, cut a 1-inch (2.5 cm) square hole out of the bottom.

#2   Use a small piece of modeling clay to support each card so that it stands upright.

#3   Align the index cards so that the holes are in a straight line.

#4   Turn off the lights and place the flashlight on the table. Observe how the light passes through all the holes and out the other side.

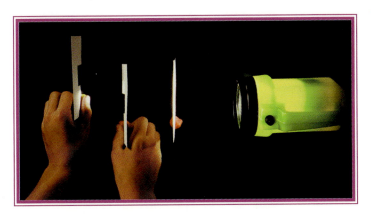

#5   Rearrange the index cards so that the holes are no longer aligned. What happens to the beam of light from the flashlight?

#6 Cut rectangular-shaped holes in the shoe box.

#7 Position the flashlight so that it shines through the hole and into the shoe box.

#8 Place one of the mirrors at the corner across from the hole and support it with a piece of modeling clay. What happens to the beam of light?

#9 Place the other mirror in the corner across from the other hole and support it with a piece of modeling clay.

#10 Adjust the two mirrors so that the light that enters the small hole exits through the large hole. When the mirrors are adjusted, secure them in place with tape and more modeling clay. Place the lid on the shoe box and tape it shut.

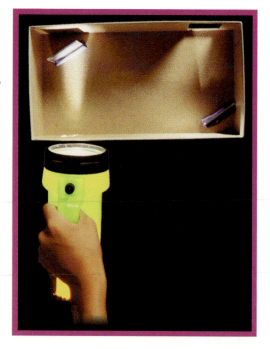

How Light Travels

#11 The device you have just con-structed is a periscope.

Analyzing Your Results

#1 What did the first five steps of the experiment tell you about the path of light?

#2 Make a diagram of the light path in the periscope. Does the light travel in a straight line?

#3 What changes the direction of the light path?

#4 Hold a book up in front of a mirror. What do you notice about the image in the mirror?

#5 Look through your periscope. Do you see a mirror image or a correct image? How can you explain your observation?

For Further Investigation

Use additional mirrors to bend light several more times. Is there a limit to the number of mirrors you could use?

2 Refraction

As you have seen, when light strikes a reflective surface, the light waves are reflected, or bounce off at an angle. When light strikes a surface that lets it pass at an angle, the light changes its speed and its direction of travel. This change in direction is called refraction.

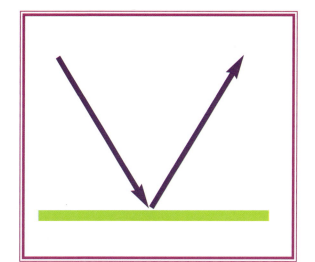

Light Striking a Surface

Different materials affect the speed and direction change differently, causing light to change speed and direction. The angle at which the light changes is called the angle of refraction. In this experiment, you will explore how light is refracted as it passes through the contact between air and water.

What You Need

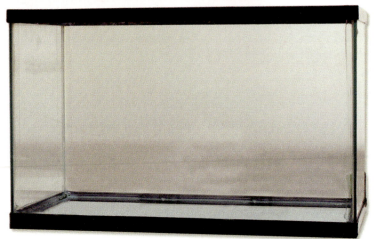

An aquarium or bucket

A coffee cup

A glass

A coin

A pencil

Marbles

What You'll Do

#1 Fill the glass with water and place the pencil in the glass so that it sticks out of the top. What do you notice about the pencil when you look at the glass from the side?

Refraction

#2   Place the coin in the coffee cup. Position your head so that the coin is just out of your view. While keeping that position, carefully pour water into the cup. Pour the water in slowly to keep from disturbing the position of the coin. What happened as you poured water into the cup?

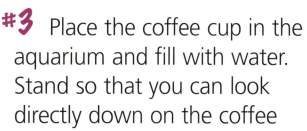

#3   Place the coffee cup in the aquarium and fill with water. Stand so that you can look directly down on the coffee cup. Drop a marble down into the aquarium and into the coffee cup. If you do not succeed, try again until you do.

#4   Move so that you are looking into the aquarium at an angle. Again, try to drop a marble into the coffee cup. If you do not succeed the first time, continue trying. Is it easier to drop marbles into the cup when looking directly down or at an angle?

#5 While still looking at the aquarium at an angle, hold a marble just under the surface of the water and try to drop it into the coffee cup. Is this easier or harder than the other ways you have tried?

Analyzing Your Results

#1 Based on your observations of the pencil in the glass and dropping the marble into the coffee cup in the aquarium, how can you explain what happened with the coin in the coffee cup?

Refraction

#2 Some ancient peoples hunted fish with spears or bows and arrows. In order to spear the fish, they would place the tip of the spear or arrow under the surface of the water. Explain why you think this would help.

For Further Investigation

#1 Use a protractor to measure the angle at which the pencil appears to bend. Line up the baseline of the protractor with the pencil to measure the angle.

#2 Substitute different liquids for the water and measure the angle again. Are the angles the same for all liquids tested?

#3 Repeat dropping the marble into the cup from different angles. Does the angle at which you look into the water make any difference?

3 The Colors of Light

Light is part of the electromagnetic spectrum. The electromagnetic spectrum is made up of energy traveling at different wavelengths.

A very narrow band of the electromagnetic spectrum is called visible light. Visible light is the light that we can see. If you have ever seen a rainbow, you have seen the colors that make up visible light.

All of these colors are blended together into what we call white light. It is possible to separate all the colors in white light so that we can see them. Each different color of light has its own wavelength. At each end of the color spectrum are other wavelengths that we cannot see. Even though we cannot see these other wavelengths, we can feel their effects. Infrared and ultraviolet are wavelengths on either side of the visible spectrum. Infrared light is felt as warmth, whereas ultraviolet light causes sunburns.

As you have seen, light is refracted as it

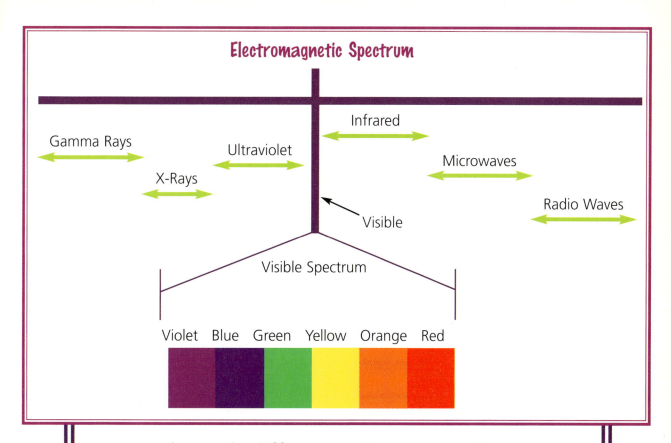

Electromagnetic Spectrum

Gamma Rays

X-Rays

Ultraviolet

Infrared

Microwaves

Radio Waves

Visible

Visible Spectrum

Violet   Blue   Green   Yellow   Orange   Red

passes through different substances. The amount that light is refracted depends on its wavelength. Because each wavelength of light travels through a substance at a different speed, it is possible to separate white light into all of its component colors.

In this activity, you will construct a water prism to separate the different wavelengths of visible light from sunlight. You will compare sunlight with the light from a flashlight. Then you will explore the spectra of different colors of light.

What You Need

- A shallow pan
- A small mirror
- A clipboard
- A pencil
- A strong flashlight
- Balloons (assorted colors)
- White paper

The Color of Light

What You'll Do

#1 Fill the pan with water and place it in direct sunlight.

#2 Place the mirror in the water at an angle facing the sun.

#3 Wait until the water becomes still and hold up the sheet of paper attached to the clipboard. Move it around until you see the rainbow of colors.

#4 Write down the order of the colors as they appear on the paper.

#5 Repeat this activity in a darkened room using a strong flashlight. Are the colors in the same order?

#6 Experiment with changing the color of the light from the flashlight beam by stretching different-colored balloons over the end of the flashlight.

The Color of Light

Analyzing Your Results

#1 What is the order of the colors in the spectrum from sunlight?

#2 Is the order of the colors in the spectrum the same with a flashlight?

#3 Describe how changing the color of the light affected the spectrum.

#4 Explain how the water prism works in terms of reflection and refraction.

#5 What do you think this has to do with the formation of rainbows?

For Further Investigation

#1 Experiment with different light sources. Try using incandescent, fluorescent, and halogen lights.

#2 Set up the clipboard on a stand. Repeat the activity, and sketch the actual sizes of the different colors on the spectrum. Experiment with different light sources and identify any differences in the spectra they produce.

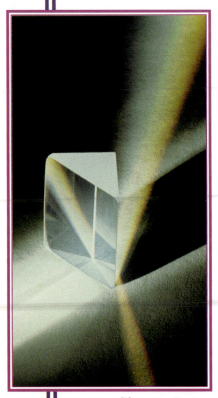

Glass prism

#3 If you have access to a glass prism, you can explore the presence of electromagnetic radiation that falls outside the visible spectrum. Set up the prism in sunlight so that it projects a spectrum onto paper. Use a thermometer to measure the temperatures of the different colors. Be sure that you move the thermometer beyond each side of the visible spectrum.

4 Properties of Light

You have seen that light travels in waves and in straight lines. You have also learned that light is made up of different colors. In this activity, you will explore another one of the properties of light.

Most light that you have seen is called incoherent light. Incoherent light is made up of many different wavelengths. Unlike the waves on the ocean, these different wavelengths travel randomly. Light that is made up of only one wavelength with all the waves traveling together is called coherent light. A laser is an example of coherent light.

Coherent light source

Incoherent light source

Most of the light sources that you're familiar with produce incoherent light. Lightbulbs produce light by passing an electric current through a filament. The filament glows and emits light.

A laser, on the other hand, produces a narrow, uniform, high-intensity beam. High-powered lasers deliver incredible amounts of energy in the beam and it can be used to vaporize the hardest and most heat-resistant materials.

In this experiment, you will explore a low-powered coherent light source and an incoherent light source.

IMPORTANT

Even though the laser used in this activity is low powered, care should be taken when using it. Do not shine the laser in your eyes or in anyone else's eyes.

Properties of Light

What You Need

- A small flashlight
- A laser pointer
- A ruler
- A tape measure, yardstick, or meterstick

What You'll Do

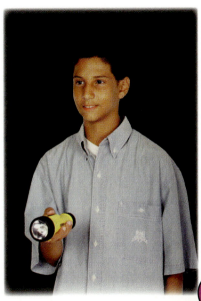

#1 In a darkened room, shine the flashlight on the wall from 3 feet (1 m) away. Focus the beam of the flashlight so that it is at its maximum brightness.

27

Distance from wall	Diameter of unfocused beam	Diameter of focused beam

#2 Have a friend measure the diameter of the brightest part of the beam. Record your measurement in your data table.

#3 Move the flashlight out to 6 feet (2 m) from the wall.

#4 Do not refocus the beam. Measure the diameter of the brightest part of the beam and record your measurement in your data table.

#5   Now, focus the beam of the flashlight and measure the diameter of the brightest part of the beam. Record your measurement in the data table.

#6   Repeat steps 3 and 4 at 9 feet (3 m) from the wall. Continue moving the flashlight back in 3-foot (1 m) intervals as many times as possible.

#7   Repeat steps 1 through 4 with the laser pointer. There is no need to focus the laser as you move it farther back from the wall.

Be careful not to look directly into the laser beam and do not shine it in anyone else's eyes.

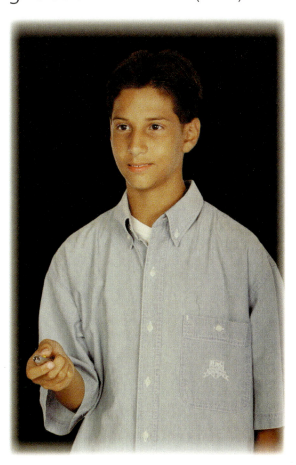

Analyzing Your Results

#1 What happened to the flashlight beam as you moved the flashlight farther from the wall?

#2 How did the intensity of the flashlight beam change as you moved the flashlight farther from the wall?

#3 How did the flashlight beam differ from the beam of the laser?

For Further Investigation

#1 Project the laser beam over a distance of 100 feet (30 m) and measure the diameter of the beam. Increase the distance as much as possible.

5 Images and Lenses

Light travels in parallel waves. When these parallel waves pass through a lens, such as a magnifying glass, the waves are bent. Since the waves are no longer traveling parallel, they end up meeting at a certain point from the lens. Where the light waves meet, they form an image. An image can be seen either closer to or farther from the lens, but it will be out of focus. A clear, focused image occurs only at a point called the focal length of the lens.

In this experiment, you will explore how a magnifying glass forms an image on a screen of white paper. You will measure the distance from an object to the magnifying glass and from the magnifying glass to the image. You will experiment with different positions of the object to see how it affects the image. Then you will find the focal length of the lens.

Experiment #4

What You Need

- White paper
- A magnifying glass
- A yardstick or meterstick
- A flashlight
- Black construction paper
- Tape
- Modeling clay
- A ruler
- Graph paper

What You'll Do

#1 Trace the top of the flashlight on black construction paper and cut out the circle.

#2 Fold the circle of construction paper in half and cut a triangle out of the edge as shown in the diagram.

#3 Unfold the construction paper, and tape a small square of white tissue paper over the triangle.

#4 Tape the construction paper over the lens of the flashlight. The triangle will be used as the object for the next part of the experiment. Measure the height of the triangle.

#5 Lay the yardstick or meterstick on a flat surface in a darkened room. Place the flashlight and magnifying glass on pieces of modeling clay for supports. Fold the sheet of white paper in three so that it can stand up without support.

#6 Set the distance between the flashlight and the magnifying glass at exactly 8 inches (or 20 cm). Adjust the position of the screen until the image is sharp. Record the image distance in a data table. Use a ruler to measure the height of the image on the screen.

Object distance	Image distance	Object size
8 inches (20 cm)		
10 inches (25 cm)		

Images and Lenses

#7 Repeat step 6 six times changing the object distance from 8 inches to 20 inches in 2-inch increments (20 cm to 70 cm in 5-cm increments). You will need to readjust the screen for each change in the object distance. Record all the distances in the data table. What happens to the image size as the object distance increases?

Analyzing Your Results

#1 In steps 6 and 7, what happened to the image distance as the object distance increased?

#2 Make a graph of your data. Let the vertical axis represent the image distance and let the horizontal axis represent the object distance. Do not connect the points with lines. Do the data points appear in a straight line or a curve?

For Further Investigation

#1 Repeat the activity using a different magnifying glass. How do the results compare when two different magnifying glasses are used?

#2 Set up your device so that you can view a distant, well-lighted object such as a tree or building. What is the image distance? How does this compare to the other image distances that you measured?

#3 The mathematical formula that describes simple optics is:

$$\frac{1}{\text{(object distance)}} + \frac{1}{\text{(image distance)}} = \frac{1}{\text{(focal length)}}.$$

Find the focal length of your lens from your experimental data.

6 Seeing Faraway Things

When you think of astronomy, you probably think of someone looking through a telescope. The most common telescope is the refractor telescope. The refractor telescope is a long tube with a lens, called the objective lens, at one end and an eyepiece at the other. When you look through the eyepiece, you see a magnified image. Telescopes are used to observe distant objects such as craters on the moon, the rings of Saturn, or stars.

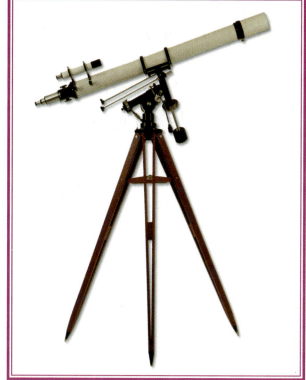

   As you found in the previous experiment, light passes through a lens and then forms an image. The same thing happens with the objective lens of a telescope. It is the telescope's eyepiece that magnifies the image.

In the telescope that you will build in this experiment, you will first need to find where the image is formed by the objective lens so that the eyepiece can magnify it. The telescope that you will build is open instead of a tube. The open design of this telescope lets you see where the image is formed and how it is magnified. The lens of an inexpensive pair of reading glasses serves as the objective lens, and a magnifying glass serves as the eyepiece.

Seeing Faraway Things

What You Need

- Reading glasses (drugstore reading glasses; choose a pair with low numbers)
- A magnifying glass
- A lamp
- Masking tape
- Wax paper or thin typing paper

What You'll Do

#1 Tape the reading glasses to the back of a chair. Make sure that one lens sticks out beyond the chair. This lens will serve as the objective lens for your telescope.

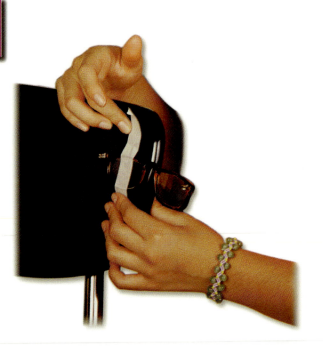

#2 Place the chair with the objective lens 12 feet (4 m) from the lamp. Turn on the lamp and turn off all other lights in the room.

#3 Hold up the sheet of paper in front of the objective lens (on the side opposite the lamp) to serve as a screen. Move the paper until the image projected by the lens is sharpest. This is the focal point for the objective lens.

#4 Have a friend hold the paper for you at the focal point. Face the back of the paper and look through it at the image. Use the magnifying glass to make the image larger.

Adjust the position of the magnifying glass until the image is sharpest. The magnifying glass serves as the eyepiece.

#5 Ask your friend to move the paper as you continue to look through the eyepiece. How does the image look now?

#6 Look at other objects near the lamp. You may need to move the eyepiece to the left, right, up, or down.

Experiment #6

Analyzing Your Results

#1 Why do you think the white paper was used as a screen to determine where the image was located?

#2 Why do you think you want a low-powered objective lens?

#3 How could you make the image that you see larger?

#4 What do you think would happen if you used the magnifying glass as the objective lens and the reading glasses as the eyepiece? Try it and find out.

Seeing Far Away Things

For Further Investigation

#1   With the paper in place, measure the distance from the objective lens to the screen and between the screen and the eyepiece. Set up your telescope so that you can see a distant object outside. Measure the distances again. How did they change?

#2   Construct a telescope using lenses and a mailing tube. Use the telescope to observe distant objects, the moon, or even planets. Do not use your telescope to look at the sun.

glossary

coherent light   Light that has waves of similar intensity and wavelengths that travel together.

electromagnetic spectrum   The entire range of electro-magnetic waves, from very long wavelengths to very short wavelengths.

eyepiece   The lens in a series of lenses that is closest to the eye.

image   The optical reproduction of an object.

incoherent light   Light that is made up of many different wavelengths and intensities of light.

infrared   An invisible part of the electromagnetic spectrum that we feel as heat.

laser   A device that emits an intense, coherent beam of light.

lens   A piece of glass or other transparent material that bends light waves to make an image of an object

medium   Material through which waves pass.

objective lens   The lens in a series of lenses that first receives incoming light from a distant object.

prism   Something that bends light and separates it into its different components.

reflection   Waves that are turned back or thrown back.

refraction   Waves that are bent from a straight line.

ultraviolet   Invisible waves in the electromagnetic spectrum just beyond the visible violet light.

visible light   The narrow band of the electromagnetic spec-trum that we can see.

wave   A disturbance moving through a medium by which energy is transferred from one particle to another.

wavelength   The distance between the tops of waves.

resources

These Web sites will help you find out more about light and optics.

Cool Science for Curious Kids
http://www.hhmi.org/coolscience

Cyberspace Middle School—Science Fair Projects
http://www.scri.fsu.edu/~dennisl/special/sf_projects.html

Exploratorium
http://www.exploratorium.edu

The Franklin Institute
http://sln.fi.edu

Mad Scientist Network
http://www.madsci.org

National Science Foundation: Science in the Home
http://www.her.nsf.gov/ehr/ehr/science_home/html/default.html

Newton Ask a Scientist
http://newton.dep.anl.gov/aasquest.htm

The Science Club
http://www.halcyon.com/sciclub

Science Fair Project Ideas
http://othello.mech.nwu.edu/~peshkin/scifair/index.html

Scientific American Explore!
http://www.sciam.com/explorations

Smithsonian Institute
http://www.si.edu

for further reading

Berger. Melvin. *All About Light: A Do-It-Yourself Science Book*. New York: Scholastic, Inc., 1995.

Gardner, Robert. *Optics*. New York: Twenty First Century Books, 1995.

Gold-Dworkin, Heidi, and Donna Goodman Lee. *Exploring Light and Color*. New York: McGraw-Hill, 1999.

Riley, Peter. *Light and Color*. Danbury, CT: Franklin Watts, 1999.

Wood, Robert W. *Light Fundamentals: Fantastic Science Activities for Kids*. New York: McGraw-Hill, 1996.

Zubrowski, Bernie. *Mirrors: Finding Out About the Properties of Light*. New York: William Morrow & Co., 1992.

index

credits

About the Author
Allan Cobb is a freelance science writer living in Central Texas. He has written books, radio scripts, articles, and educational materials concerning different aspects of science. When not writing about science, he enjoys traveling, camping, hiking, and exploring caves.

Photo Credits
Cover photo by Scott Bauer. P.11 © CORBIS/Owen Franken; p.17 © CORBIS/Michael Freeman; p.24 © SUPERSTOCK; P.36 © CORBIS/Roger Ressmeyer. All other photos by Scott Bauer.

Design and Layout
Laura Murawski

Consulting Editor
Amy Haugesag

Metric Conversions
To convert measurements in U.S. units into metric units, use the following formulas:

1 inch = 2.54 centimeters (cm)	1 ounce = 28.35 grams (g)
1 foot = 0.30 meters (m)	1 gallon = 3.79 liters (l)
1 mile = 1.609 kilometers (km)	1 pound = 453.59 grams (g)